IN THE RAINFOREST

Penny Dowdy

Created by Q2AMedia

www.q2amedia.com

Copyright © Leopard Learning 2009
www.leopardlearning.com

Editor William Wagner
Publishing Director Chester Fisher
Client Service Manager Santosh Vasudevan
Project Manager Shekhar Kapur
Art Director Sumit Charles
Designer Joita Das
Image Researcher Poulomi Basu

10 9 8 7 6 5 4 3 2 1

ISBN: 978-81-905723-4-7

Printed in China

Picture Credit
t=top b=bottom l=left r=right

Cover Images: Front: Michaeljun: Dreamstime.

Back: Winfried Wisniewski: Photolibrary. Steve Heap: Shutterstock.

Half Title: Joyce Mar: Shutterstock

Content Images: James Steidl: Shutterstock. Brandon Seidel: Shutterstock. Liga Lauzuma/ Shutterstock.

4-5 Antonio Jorge Nunes: Shutterstock. **6** Philip Lange: Shutterstock. **7t** Serg64: Shutterstock. **8-9** Steve Bloom Images: Alamy. **9t** Morales: Photolibrary. **10** Kerstin Layer: Photolibrary. **11** Juniors Bildarchiv: Photolibrary. **12** Jeanne White: Photo Researchers. **13t** Mike Hill: Photolibrary. **13br** Javarman: Shutterstock. **14** Theo Allofs: Corbis. **15** Lynn Stone: Photolibrary. **16-17** Doug Wechsler: Photolibrary. **17t** Merlin D. Tutle: Dinodia. **18** Jürgen + Christine Sohns: Photolibrary. **19br** Stuart Westmorland: Photolibrary. **19bl** Pakhnyushcha: Shutterstock. **20** Roy Toft: Photolibrary. **21** Phil Savoie: Naturepl.

22 Karel Gallas: Shutterstock. **23** Batman2000: Dreamstime. **24** Nicola Vernizzi: Shutterstock. **25** Jane Rix: Shutterstock. **26** Joe Mc Donald: Photolibrary. **27** Ryan M. Bolton: Shutterstock. **28-29** Uwe Roll: Photolibrary. **29t** Joe Mc Donald: Photolibrary. **30-31** Dr. Morley Read: Shutterstock. **31t** Mark Moffett: Dinodia. **32t** Wikipedia. **32b** Wikipedia. **33t** Nicole L. Michelz. **33b** Wikipedia. **34** Louiseefer: Fotolia. **35** Austin J. Stevens: Photolibrary. **36-37** Colin Jones: Photolibrary. **37t** Martin Harvey: Photolibrary. **38** Eric Gevaert: Shutterstock. **39b** Nicola Vernizzi: Shutterstock. **39t** Fedor Selivanov: Shutterstock. **40** Wikipedia.

Content

All About Rainforests

Rainforests are **ecosystems** with tall trees and a lot of rain. Some rainforests are near the **equator**, but not all of them. Even Canada and Australia have rainforests!

Every rainforest has warm weather all year. The weather does not change from one season to another.

Rainforests are the oldest ecosystem on Earth. Some trees in the South American rainforest are around a thousand years old!

Arctic Ocean

Atlantic Ocean

Pacific Ocean

Indian Ocean

Pacific Ocean

TROPICAL RAINFORESTS OF THE WORLD
TEMPERATE RAINFORESTS OF THE WORLD

What do you know about living in the rainforest? On the following pages, you can learn and discover what the rainforest is and who lives there!

The Layers of the Rainforest

Every rainforest has a few very tall trees. These reach as tall as a 15-story building! The tops of the tallest trees create the **emergent** layer.

Below the emergent layer there are trees that are slightly shorter. Don't be fooled, as these trees are still very tall! The leaves of these trees blend together. This is called the **canopy**. Below the canopy you find some smaller trees. These may be **seedlings** of canopy trees or other types of shorter trees. Vines and other small plants grow here, too. This is called the **understory**.

FACT

The forest **floor** gets almost no sunlight, so there are few plants there. **Decaying** leaves, fungi, swamps, rivers, and streams cover the forest floor.

Emergent Layer

Canopy

Understory

Forest Floor

▲ *A huge variety of animals are found at all levels of the rainforest.*

7

Apes

When you think of rainforest animals, you may think of apes. Apes are not monkeys. How do you tell the difference? Most apes do not have tails. Monkeys do.

Orangutan

Orangutans are apes. They sleep, nest, eat, and live almost their entire life in trees. Males like to live alone, not in communities like the females and children. Orangutans eat fruits, leaves, and bugs.

An orangutan's arms help it move among branches.

Loud howls let other male orangutans know that there is already a male in the area.

Gorilla

Gorillas are also a type of ape. They live in **communities** of up to 30 gorillas. They can grow to over 400 pounds. These big **primates** can climb trees, but prefer to live on the ground. Gorillas only eat plants. They bark, hoot, and roar. They also pound their chests to show their power.

Gorillas are led by an older male, called a silverback.

Spider and Howler Monkeys

Remember that monkeys and apes are not the same kind of animal. Monkeys cannot swing by their arms from trees, like orangutans do. Instead, they run along the tree tops.

Spider Monkey

Adult spider monkeys are only about 1-2 feet tall, on top of the length of the tail. Unlike most other monkeys, these monkeys have no thumbs! They sleep and hunt in small groups. At times, they stay in larger groups of 2-3 dozen, called troops. Spider monkeys eat nuts, fruits, bird eggs, and spiders.

A spider monkey spends almost its entire life in treetops.

Group calls can be heard up to three miles away!

Howler monkeys have thumbs like most other monkeys.

Howler Monkey

Howler monkeys are named for the loud sound they make. They grow 2-3 feet long, plus their tails. Howler monkeys use their tails for grabbing and balance. They eat leaves, and live in troops of 1-2 dozen.

FACT

Have you ever watched a movie with monkeys shouting in a jungle? Chances are the sound is the call of a howler monkey.

Jaguars and Ocelots

Cats, both big and small, call the South American rainforest, home. Do you know the difference between big cats and small cats? It is not about size! Only big cats can roar, and only small cats can purr.

A jaguar can jump up to 20 feet.

The ocelot's eyes collect light even at night, so hunting is easier.

An ocelot has a spotted coat, like many jaguars do.

Jaguar

A jaguar is a big cat that also happens to be large. They grow to be between 120 and 300 pounds. Jaguars are also called panthers, and can run up to 40 miles an hour. These cats are great swimmers. They like to hunt at night, and then take their **prey** into trees for protection while they eat.

Ocelot

An ocelot is a small cat, only about twice the size of a housecat. Ocelots climb trees and sleep there during the day. They hunt at night. Ocelots hunt on land and in trees. They cannot chew. Instead they tear their food and swallow it whole.

Capybaras and Tapirs

These two rainforest animals do not look like they have much in common. However, both animals are **herbivores**. Both have unusual noses. And both can swim!

Capybara

Rats, mice, and hamsters are all **rodents.** The capybara is the biggest rodent in the world. They are about the same size as a large dog! A capybara spends a lot of time in the water. It can even sleep in the water with its nose above the surface to breathe. They live in groups of 10-30, led by a strong male.

Adult capybaras can weigh as much as 100 pounds.

Humans live in the rainforest, too. Some rainforest groups have never been in contact with people from outside of their rainforest.

FACT

Tapirs use their noses like an elephant's trunk.

A tapir's body is shaped like a very large watermelon!

Tapir

Tapirs are the largest land mammals in the South American rainforest. These animals grow 3-4 feet tall, and weigh over 500 pounds. Tapirs like to live alone and usually run to avoid danger. If they must defend themselves, they use sharp teeth to bite.

Bats

Bats are **mammals**, not birds. They are the only mammal that can fly. There are more bats than any other mammal in the rainforest.

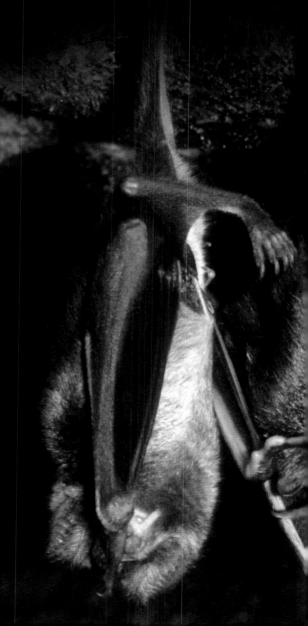

▶| *Vampire bats sleep upside-down in groups of up to a thousand, called a colony.*

Vampire Bat

Vampire bats have a dangerous reputation. These bats are about 3½ inches tall and seven inches across with their wings open. Vampire bats survive only on blood, and can double their weight in one meal! However, they are able to drink blood without hurting their prey.

Hog-nosed Bat

The hog-nosed bat is the world's smallest bat. It weighs less than a penny and grows only 1-1.5 inches tall. Hog-nose bats sleep in colonies of 4-5 bats. These bats fly only at dawn and dusk, for a total of an hour a day. They eat small insects.

Its wings let this bat hover like a hummingbird or bumblebee.

The hog-nosed bat has its name because its face looks like a pig.

FACT

Bats are very important to an ecosystem. Insect-eaters control the population of bugs. Fruit eaters spread seeds so that new plants can grow.

17

Macaws
and **Toucans**

Rainforests are full of birds, from the lowest to the highest branches. Many of these birds have developed special qualities, which help them live there.

▶| *The brightly colored macaws can imitate any sound.*

Macaws

Macaws are found in the rainforests of Central and South America. They have long tails, but not too many feathers, as they would get in the way while flying. They have four toes, two in front and two behind on each foot, to grip branches better. The tip of their beak is especially sharp, to tear the fruits and nuts they eat.

Toucan

In the rainforest, if you suddenly hear a sound that goes RRRK…, you are listening to a toucan. A toucan has an enormous, bright beak, rounded tail, and a small, fat body. In some species, the beak is more than half the total length of the bird. The very strong beak is surprisingly lightweight.

The feathers are generally black, with touches of white, yellow, and scarlet.

The edges of the beak are like a saw to help break open hard fruits and nuts.

Quetzals and Birds of Paradise

The Amazon Rainforest is home to many large, colorful birds. People used to hunt the birds to get feathers for expensive clothes and hats. Native people who live in the rainforest still use the feathers in the clothes they wear. The male birds use their feathers to attract **mates**. The females are very plain!

Quetzal

A quetzal is a beautiful bird that grows about 1 ½ feet long. Males grow tail feathers up to three feet long! Quetzals eat fruits, insects, and small animals. They use their strong beaks to tear holes in hollow trees to make nests.

The name quetzal comes from the Aztec word for "stands up."

Bird of Paradise

Male birds of paradise are like other birds of the Amazon—they have very colorful feathers. Like the quetzal, these birds nest in holes in trees or on branches. Males dance for hours to **attract** females and find mates. Each type of bird of paradise has a different type of dance!

Look how plain the female bird of paradise looks compared to the male!

This male bird of paradise puts on a show to attract a mate.

Hornbills and Harpy Eagles

The rainforest provides homes to many different types of birds. Not all are beautiful. Some are just unusual.

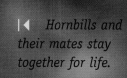

Hornbills and their mates stay together for life.

The sharp beak helps the harpy eagle eat monkeys, rodents, snakes, and lizards.

Hornbill

You can easily recognize a hornbill. A hornbill has a bump on top of its beak, called a casque. These casques help hornbills make loud calls. Some bills have edges like saws that the birds use for cutting. Hornbills eat bugs, small animals, and fruit. They live in hollows of trees.

Harpy Eagle

Harpy eagles are the heaviest and most powerful bird. They grow 3-4 feet long with a seven foot wingspan. These eagles build nests four feet deep, five feet across, and over a hundred feet off the ground! Harpy eagles are excellent hunters. They fly up to 50 miles per hour, and can carry prey in their large talons.

23

Amphibians

Scientists think that the health and number of frogs and toads show how polluted an ecosystem is. When the number of frogs or toads goes down, scientists have a clue that the ecosystem may not be healthy.

Poison Arrow Frog

Brightly-colored poison arrow frogs eat tiny insects in the rainforest. These frogs get their name from the poison that is found on their skin. Native people can gather the poison to make poison darts. Some poison arrow frogs have a little poison, but others are very poisonous. Other rainforest frogs copy the colors of the poison arrow frog so they can pretend to be poisonous to frighten away **predators**.

The male poison arrow frog watches over his eggs until they hatch into tadpoles.

Cane toads release a milky liquid that is poisonous.

The cane toad's back feet are webbed, but its front feet are not.

Cane Toad

Cane toads are big! They weigh up to four pounds and can grow nine inches long. Cane toads eat lizards, frogs, birds, fish, mice, bees, worms, beetles, and even smaller cane toads.

Snakes

Many types of snakes live in the rainforest. They live on the ground, in the trees, and in the water.

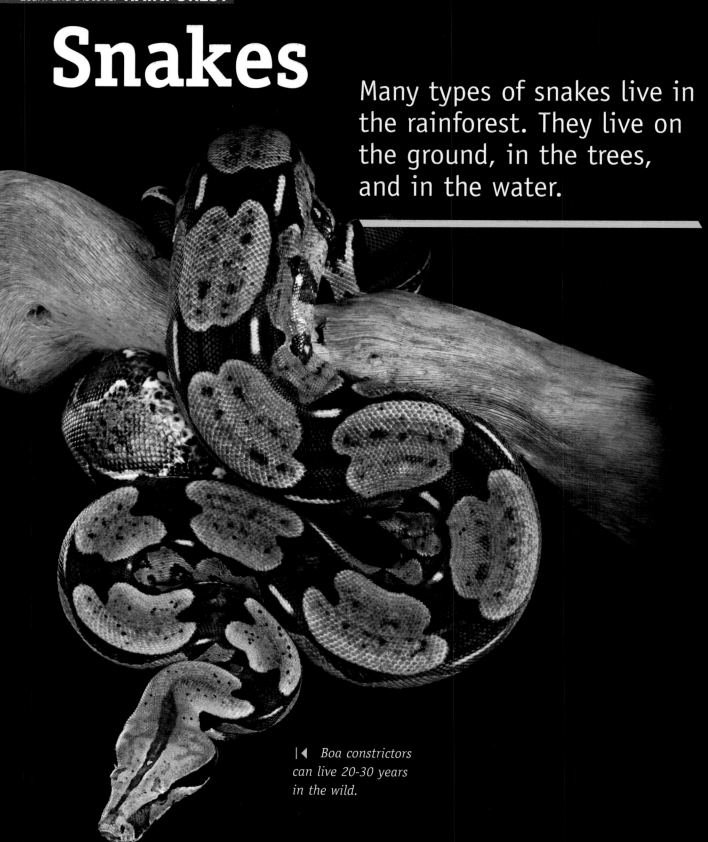

|◀ *Boa constrictors can live 20-30 years in the wild.*

Boa Constrictor

Boa constrictors are large snakes that hang from the branches of trees. They hunt at night, looking for other animals high in the air. Their favorite food is bats. The boa constrictors catch them as they fly by. They will eat other small animals, too. Boa constrictors are not poisonous. They squeeze their prey to death.

Anacondas are in the same family as boa constrictors. They are also the largest snake in the world, growing over 20 feet long. They have jaws that open wide to swallow prey whole, including jaguars and alligators.

FACT

The snake uses its tongue to tell when temperature changes. They can even sense when warm-blooded animals are near.

Fer-de-Lance

The fer-de-lance is a highly poisonous snake. It kills more people in the Americas than any other snake! The fer-de-lance lives on the ground, but it can climb and swim, too. This snake strikes so fast it is almost impossible to see

The fer-de-lance's

More Reptiles

Lizards and alligators are in the same family as snakes. **Reptiles** usually live in warm areas like South American rainforests. Some are smaller than a human finger. Others are bigger than an adult human.

Black Caiman

The black caiman is the largest type of alligator, over 16 feet long. It hunts at night, so its color helps with **camouflage**. Caimans have great hearing and sight, which help it hunt. They eat fish and other animals that live in or near rivers and swamps. Females build nests for their eggs close together so they may protect each other and the eggs.

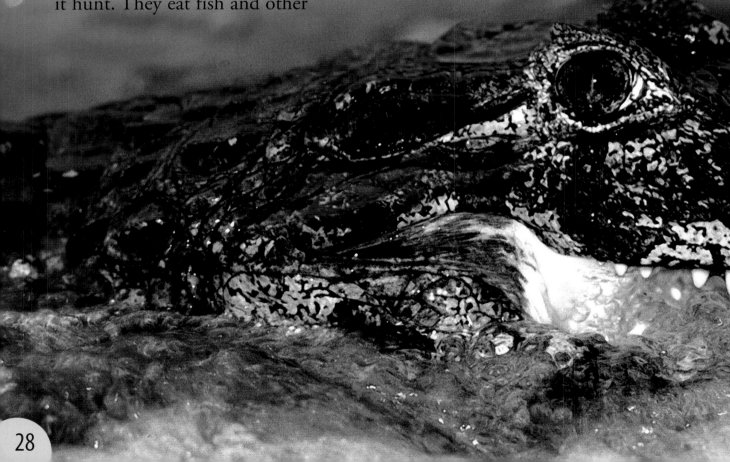

The basilisk is sometimes called a crested lizard because of the crest on its head.

The basilisk can run five feet per second.

▶| *The basilisk prefers to run on water.*

Basilisk

The basilisk is much smaller, only two feet long. These lizards hang in branches above rivers and streams. When the basilisk is threatened, it drops into the water and runs across the surface. They eat plants and small fish and animals.

◀| *The black caiman's mouth is about two feet long!*

FACT

Can you imagine any animal that would not fear a piranha? The Black caiman does not. Piranhas are this alligator's favorite food.

29

Ants

There are many different types of animals living in the South American rainforest. Did you know there are more insects in the rainforest than any other kind of animal?

Leaf-Cutter Ant

The leaf-cutter ant takes more leaves from the rainforest than any other animal.

Leaf-cutter ants have amazing strength. They can carry 20 times their body weight. Leaf-cutter ants cut up leaves, but do not eat them. They leave the cut pieces in their nests. The leaves then grow fungus, which the leaf-cutter ants eat.

Azteca Ant

Azteca ants live in a Cecropia tree. The tree and ants help each other. The ants live in the hollows of the tree. They also eat sweet drops of nectar and insects from the tree. In return, the ants attack anything that threatens the tree. A team of ants hold the intruder down, carry it, and throw it off the tree.

▲ *Up to 20 queens may set up colonies in one tree.*

Leaf cutter ants have powerful jaws that cut through stems and leaves of plants growing in the rainforest.

31

Beetles and Butterflies

As you saw with birds, the males are colorful to attract very plain females. Some male and female insects have differences, too.

MALE

The wings contain poison that the insect ate while it was a caterpillar.

Queen Alexandra's Birdwing Butterfly

The Queen Alexandra's birdwing butterfly is huge. It measures over a foot across when its wings are open. Females are brown, but males are very colorful. They fly high in the rainforest and may never touch the ground.

FEMALE

Hercules Beetle

The Hercules beetle is the world's largest beetle. Males can be 7 inches long! Males also have horns used for fighting. Females have no horns and do not fight. The beetles live longer as **larva**, eating rotting wood. It takes years for the larva to grow into beetles.

FEMALE

Insects can be endangered, just as other animals can. The Queen Alexandra's birdwing butterfly is an endangered species. People used to capture them to keep in a butterfly collection. This is now illegal.

FACT

◀ *Notice how different the male and female look.*

MALE

Spiders and Scorpions

Spiders and scorpions are found all over the world. They are not insects. You can tell by counting legs. Insects have six, spiders and scorpions have eight.

▶ *The Goliath Bird-eating spider throws hairs from its legs at predators. The hairs have hooks that latch onto skin and cause a bad rash.*

The tail can inject
a deadly venom.

A pinch from this
scorpion can hurt, too!

Goliath Bird-Eating Spider

The goliath bird-eating spider grows as large as a dinner plate (11 inches.) The spider's name tells you what it eats: birds. However, it can eat frogs, snakes, and rodents, too. With such big meals, these spiders can go for a month without eating. The goliath also makes a hissing sound with the hairs on its legs to scare away predators.

Brazilian Yellow Scorpion

The Brazilian yellow scorpion is much smaller, at only 2½ inches long. Its small size does not mean it is not dangerous. This scorpion has a very deadly venom. It eats insects, spiders, and worms. Mother scorpions can **reproduce** without a father.

Threats to the
Rainforests

South American rainforests have amazing plants and animals. However, rainforests all over the world are threatened and even shrinking.

Threats to Plants

Many plants are disappearing from rainforests. Companies cut trees down for timber. Villages clear plants off the land to make room for farms and ranches. As cities near rainforests grow, builders cut trees and plants down to make room for new homes. The rainforest is rich with oil, so companies cut trees to drill.

Cutting down trees damages all living things in rainforests.

36

Threats to Animals

Without the rainforest plants, most rainforest animals would lose their homes. The loss of habitat forces animals to different environments. If the animals cannot find food and shelter, they may not survive. Many rainforest animals are hunted, too. People hunt them for sport. In many cases, hunters are breaking the law.

▲ *People living in the rainforest depend on the plants and animals to survive.*

Threats to People

Many people call rainforests home. These groups live off the land of the rainforest. They use their knowledge of plants and animals of the rainforests in their art, medicines, and communities. When the rainforests are destroyed the people lose their homes.

Glossary

attract to interest or appeal to

camouflage the ability to hide in one's environment using the way one looks

canopy a shade that hangs over something

community a group of living things that live together

decay to rot or come apart

ecosystem a system of living things that share an environment

emergent newly formed

equator an imaginary circle around the middle of the earth

floor the ground surface

herbivore an animal that eats only plants

larva an early form of an insect, looks like a worm

mammal a warm blooded animal who nurses its young

mate one of a pair of animals that will produce young

predator an animal that hunts other animals

prey an animal that is hunted by another

primate mammal with hands and feet that grip and large brains

reproduce to create a child or young animal

reptile cold blooded land animals that have scales and lay eggs

rodent small mammals with sharp, gnawing teeth

seedling a young plant

understory a plant between a canopy and the ground

Index

Webfinder

http://science.howstuffworks.com/conservation-issues/rainforest.htm
http://www.ran.org
http://www.rainforesteducation.com/
http://www.blueplanetbiomes.org/rainforest.htm
http://www.nature.org/rainforests/